JOURNEY TO THE PLANETS

JOURNEY TO THE PLANETS

BY PATRICIA LAUBER

CROWN PUBLISHERS, INC.
New York

FOR PIP

PICTURE CREDITS

All photographs courtesy of National Aeronautics and Space Administration
except the following:

Hale Observatories: 14, 17, 18, 38
U.S. Air Force: 2 (*right*)
U.S. Geological Survey, Department of the Interior: 10, 11
Yerkes Observatory, University of Chicago: 29, 85

Text copyright © 1982 by Patricia Lauber
Manufactured in the United States of America
Published simultaneously in Canada by General Publishing Company Limited
10 9 8 7 6 5 4 3 2 1

The text of this book is set in 14 point Bodoni Book.
The illustrations are black-and-white photographs.

Library of Congress Cataloging in Publication Data
Lauber, Patricia.
Journey to the Planets
Includes index.
Summary: Explores the planets of our solar system,
highlighting the prominent features of each.
1. Planets—Juvenile literature.   [1. Planets]
I. Title.
QB602.L258   1982   523.4   82-1426
ISBN 0-517-54477-6   AACR2

CONTENTS

Earth, as photographed by APOLLO 17 *astronauts, from the Mediterranean sea (top) to the polar ice cap of Antarctica. Nearly the whole coastline of Africa can be seen, with the Arabian peninsula to the northeast of Africa. The large island is the Malagasy Republic.*

EARTH

THE BLUE PLANET

S E E N from space, Earth is a beautiful big blue marble marked with swirls and threads and patches of white. A close look shows that the white patches are polar ice. The swirls and threads are clouds, moving in ever-changing patterns in the planet's atmosphere. Behind them continents rise from blue seas that cover much of the surface. And the continents are cloaked in colors that change with the seasons. To observers from another solar system, Earth would appear a most interesting planet. The atmosphere, the clouds, the seas, the changing colors would all hint that Earth might be a planet of life.

Except perhaps for a spacecraft launch, signs of life are invisible from space. Even the changing colors of the continents need not be a sign of plant life. They could be caused by dust storms or by chemicals that are affected by light or heat. Still, alien observers would consider Earth a promising place for close study, because there are many things about our planet that make it suitable for life.

LOOKING FOR INTELLIGENT LIFE

What signs of intelligent life might alien observers see on Earth? The most likely would be changes made in the landscape. If there are intelligent beings on the planet, perhaps they are builders who have put up large structures, raised cities, dug canals, built bridges and roads. If so, observers should see signs of regular geometric patterns imposed on the land.

The first photographs of a coastal area are sharp and clear. But even when they are pieced together into this picture, they show no signs of life, intelligent or otherwise.

But at night something interesting happens. Lights appear. Are they the lights of cities? Or are they some kind of natural light—rocks that glow in the dark or masses of giant fireflies?

Another camera with a different lens takes more detailed pictures, but even when they are put together, there is still no sign of life.

With still more detailed pictures, patterns suddenly spring into view. They show roads, streets, buildings, bridges, docks, boats. All must be the handiwork of intelligent beings, past or present—the alien observers have discovered New York City and nearby New Jersey.

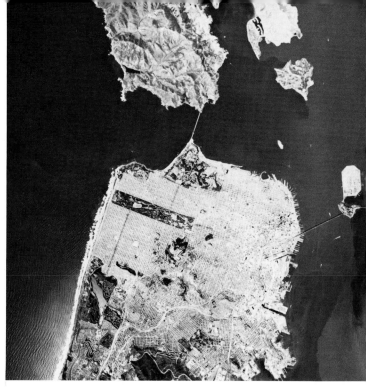

Now the cameras bring into focus towns and cities in many places. Here, on the far side of the same continent, a peninsula is revealed to have streets, buildings, bridges, a harbor, docks, boats—the aliens have discovered San Francisco.

Earth is the third planet out from the star we call our sun. It travels around the sun in a path, or orbit, that is slightly oval. On the average, Earth is 93 million miles from the sun, and that is a good distance, neither so close that our planet broils nor so far away that it freezes. Earth is the right distance from the sun for our kind of life.

That life must have fairly even temperatures. It cannot survive changes of hundreds or thousands of degrees. On Earth such changes do not occur. Its surface is gently warmed and cooled, both daily and during the year.

Daily warming and cooling occur because the earth spins on its axis, an imaginary line that runs through its center from the North Pole to the South. Parts of the earth are warmed by the sun's rays by day, then cooled as they move away from the rays and into night. As the earth's spinning continues, they travel back into daylight and warmth.

The earth also has seasons, because its axis is slightly tilted. As the earth travels around its orbit, each pole is tipped toward the sun for part of the year. When the North Pole is tipped toward the sun, the Northern Hemisphere has summer. When it is tipped away from the sun, the Northern Hemisphere has winter. As the seasons change, different parts of the earth warm up or cool off.

The warming and cooling are gentle because of the atmosphere, the envelope of air that surrounds the earth. The atmosphere is one of the chief things that make the earth a planet of life. It is the air we breathe. It is a shield that protects us from dangerous rays given off by the sun. It is a blanket that holds in some of the day's heat and keeps it from escaping at night. That is, the atmosphere acts like the glass in a greenhouse roof. Sunshine passes freely through the glass roof and is absorbed by plants and other materials. After a while, they begin to give off heat in the form of invisible rays called infrared. These rays cannot pass freely through glass and are trapped in the greenhouse. That is why a greenhouse is warmer than the outdoors. In the same way, the atmosphere traps infrared rays given off by the earth's surface.

Oceans cover nearly three-quarters of the earth, and they too help to keep temperatures even. The oceans absorb and store huge amounts of heat from the sun in warm seasons. They give off heat in cold seasons, warming the air.

Winds move air around, distributing heat. They carry hot air away from the tropics to colder regions. They carry cold air from polar regions to the tropics. The clouds of the atmosphere hold the water that falls as rain.

The atmosphere is held captive by Earth's gravity, the force that draws all things toward the center of the earth. The strength of gravity is determined by a body's mass, which is the amount of material in it. Earth's mass and gravity are other things that make our planet suitable for life. The gravity is strong enough to hold an atmosphere, to keep it from escaping into space.

The earth's magnetic field is also important to a planet of life. Something in the earth's core acts like a giant bar magnet. Earth has invisible magnetic lines of force that arch through space from pole to pole. Together these lines form a magnetic field around the earth. The field traps dangerous charged particles given off by the sun and other sources in space. It keeps the particles from bombarding Earth and probably making most kinds of life impossible. As it is, the earth supports many kinds of life: life of the land and sea and air.

In a way, it is strange that the earth has land—and land life, including us. Land is constantly wearing away into the oceans. It is eroded by air and water, two of the very things that make the earth a planet of life. Winds scour rock and carry off soil. Rains beat down. Prying fingers of frost crack rocks. Running streams carry off soil and fragments of rock into the oceans. Waves pound coastlines and break them down. Yet the earth is not covered by one huge ocean. It remains a planet of land and sea. The reason is that Earth is a planet of change, a planet where new land forms and mountains are thrust up.

The earth beneath our feet is basically a ball of rock covered mostly by oceans. The outside of the ball is a thin skin of rigid rock, which is called the crust. It is broken into a number of big pieces, or plates.

The plates of crust float on a deep layer of rock called the mantle. The rock of the mantle is very hot. Some of it flows, like extremely thick tar. Some earth scientists think that this hot rock keeps rising in currents, spreading out under the crust, cooling, and descending—just as water heated at the bottom of a pot rises in currents, spreads, cools, and descends. They think that the currents rise, very slowly, in pairs. Near the top of the mantle, each current turns and flows away from the other. Where currents separate, they break the crust and pull it apart in great rifts. Molten rock flows out of the rifts as lava. Over millions of years the lava builds a ridge.

We feel winds blowing hot, warm, cold. We see leaves and dust stirring in the wind. We see clouds being blown across the sky. But we do not see anything like this view of Earth, with the counterclockwise winds of a hurricane stirring clouds as if they were beaten egg whites. Winds help to distribute the sun's heat.

Where rifts open up, land masses are torn apart. Notice the jigsaw-puzzle fit of the Arabian peninsula (top) and Ethiopia and the Horn of Africa (bottom). Upwelling currents in the mantle have torn the two regions apart. A ridge-and-rift system runs through the Red Sea (left) and the Gulf of Aden (right). Someday the Horn of Africa may be torn off and turned into an island. Mast is part of the spacecraft from which photograph was taken.

Such a ridge runs through the earth's oceans. It is 40,000 miles long and hundreds of miles wide. Its tallest parts form islands such as Iceland and the Azores.

When currents cool, they turn down and plunge back into the mantle. Huge trenches in the ocean bottom mark places where currents turn down.

Pairs of currents act like giant conveyor belts. At a rate of an inch or two a year, they carry plates of crust away from each side of the ridge. New crust is added as lava pours out of the rifts and hardens. Old crust is carried back into the mantle at the trenches.

The crust under the oceans travels on these huge, slow-moving conveyor-belt currents. So do the continents, which are made of lighter, thicker rock than the ocean crust. They may drift together or tear apart.

Some 200 million years ago, the earth had just one big continent surrounded by one great ocean. Upwelling currents in the mantle tore the supercontinent in two, then tore the halves into smaller pieces. They became the continents we know today. The mid-Atlantic ridge marks the place where the Americas were once joined to Eurasia and Africa. As the continents were slowly carried away from each other, the gap between them became the Atlantic Ocean. The Atlantic is still growing at a rate of about one and a half inches a year, as the continents go on drifting apart.

We do not see this slow drift, but there are many signs of it. Where plates pull apart, earthquakes rumble and undersea volcanoes erupt along the ocean ridges. Where plates meet, volcanoes also erupt, quakes shake the earth, and whole chains of mountains may be thrust up.

The San Andreas fault, shown near the San Francisco peninsula, is a place where two plates meet. These two plates are passing each other sideways. Their edges grind together and lock in place. Strain builds up in the crust. When it becomes too great and the rock snaps, the crust moves suddenly. The result is an earthquake.

Earth scientists think that the big North American plate has overridden a small Pacific plate, producing the volcanic mountains of the northwestern United States. Here one of them, Mount St. Helens, erupts in 1980.

For example, South America is riding on a plate that is moving westward. The leading edge of that plate is in collision with an eastward-moving plate of the Pacific. The continent rides high. The Pacific plate dives under it. Where the plates collide, they buckle—and the Andes crumple up out of the crust. The mountains are made of rock from the crust and sediment from the ocean bottom—soil and rock fragments that were eroded and carried into the ocean. Mixed in with the sediment are the remains of sea creatures, which is why their fossils are often found in rocks miles up a mountain. An area where the earth's crust crumples is under great strain. Rock fractures and earthquakes occur. Rock melts and volcanoes erupt, adding lava to the mountains.

The Andes are young mountains that are still being built. So are the Rockies, the Alps, the Himalayas. All have soaring, craggy peaks, not yet worn down by wind, rain, snow, and frost. Other mountains, such as the Appalachians, are old. Their rounded, gentle slopes tell of erosion that has been going on for hundreds of millions of years. They formed during another, earlier period of drifting continents.

Volcanoes, earthquakes, and young mountain chains are signs of a restless, changing earth, a planet that is in a sense alive. Its land is worn down and rebuilt, worn down and rebuilt. And so it remains a planet of land and sea that can support many different kinds of life. It is the only such planet in our solar system.

We explore other planets to go where no human being has ever gone, to see what no human being has ever seen before. We explore them to learn about them. And we explore them to understand our planet better. Much of Earth's early history has been destroyed by erosion and by the building of new land. But clues to its past can be found among other members of the sun's family, for all were born at the same time and in the same way.

The Himalayas formed when the plate carrying India collided with the plate under Asia. The collision crumpled the earth's crust and forced up a big range of mountains in which the rock is folded, cracked, and tilted.

13

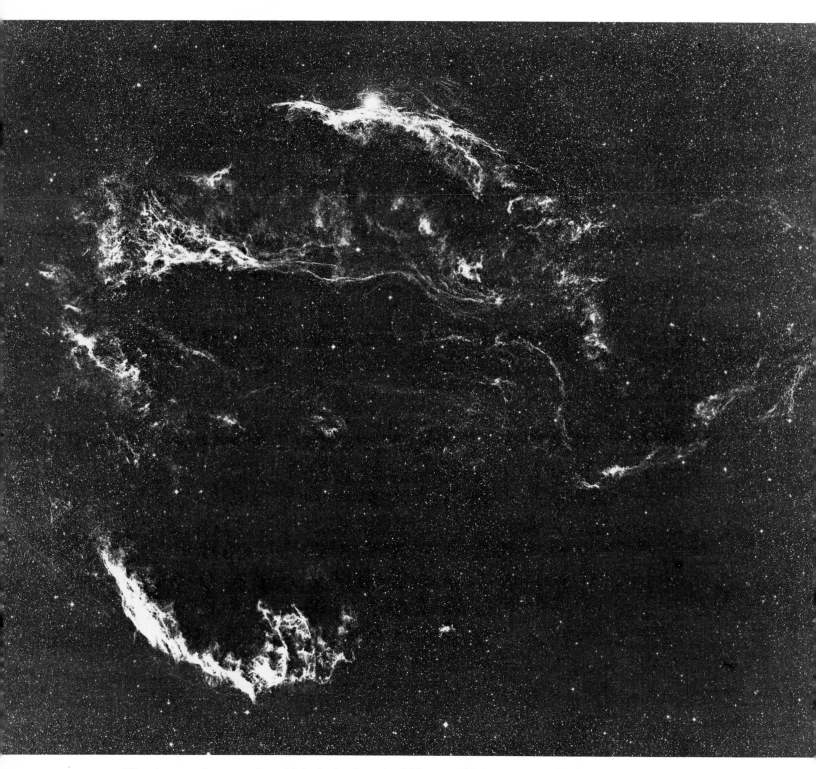

What happened to start the cold dark cloud moving? The most likely answer is shock waves from a nearby massive star that blew up at the end of its life. These wispy clouds in the constellation Cygnus are the remains of a star that blew itself apart 20,000 years ago.

A STAR IS BORN

B I L L I O N S of years ago, a vast cloud of gas and dust was floating in space. It was dark and cold and spread very thin. Then something happened, and the particles of gas and dust began to draw closer together. The cloud kept growing smaller and more dense. Slow-moving whirlpools developed within it. They caused the giant cloud to break up into smaller clouds. One of these was to become our solar system.

As our cloud went on contracting, it rotated faster and flattened into a disk. More and more gas and dust were drawn into the center of the disk, which became hotter and hotter. At last the heat and pressure were so great that atoms began to fuse. The center of the disk glowed with nuclear fires, and a new star was born.

In some such way, astronomers think, our sun came into being. Much of what happened remains a mystery, but astronomers are sure that new stars form in clouds of gas and dust. Through telescopes they can see such clouds glowing with the light of newborn stars.

As the sun was forming, something else was happening in the same spinning disk of gas and dust. Scientists think the dust grains were fluffy. When they collided, they clumped together, the way big snowflakes do. Large lumps of hot solids and gases formed. Larger lumps swept up smaller ones. As lumps gained mass, their gravitational force increased. They drew more and more matter to themselves—and grew and grew. In this way, the planets took shape.

By about 4.6 billion years ago, astronomers think, the very young planets were orbiting the very young sun.

Closest to the sun were four small planets, the ones we know as Mercury, Venus, Earth, and Mars. All were made of rocky material. And they were wrapped in atmospheres of hydrogen and helium, the main gases in the cloud. Early in their lives the four planets were so hot that they were molten. Heavier elements, such as iron, settled toward the center of each, forming a core. The core was surrounded by layers of less dense rock.

Much farther from the sun, where temperatures were lower, four giant planets formed. They are the ones we know as Jupiter, Saturn, Uranus, and Neptune. (Many astronomers think that Pluto was not then a planet.) They were made of rocky material mixed with frozen water as well as frozen methane and ammonia. They had deep atmospheres of hydrogen and helium. Jupiter seems to have formed fastest, pulling to itself huge amounts of matter. In fact, Jupiter acquired one-twelfth the mass needed to become a star, to glow with its own light. It is sometimes called a star that failed.

Between Jupiter and Mars was a belt of rocks ranging in size from huge to tiny. They were orbiting the sun and colliding with one another. We call them the asteroid belt. Asteroids may be the material of a planet that never formed, that perhaps was kept from forming by giant Jupiter's gravitation.

Once the sun started to shine, a solar wind began to blow. On Earth when we feel a wind we are feeling the movement of air molecules. A solar wind is made of atomic particles given off by the sun. Like wind on Earth, it presses on everything in its path.

When a star is young, gale winds blast off its surface. The early solar wind blew like a hurricane. It swept dust and gas out of the solar system. The small inner planets lost their original atmospheres. But the giant planets held theirs, because of their strong gravity and their great distance from the sun.

This cloud of gas and dust in the constellation of Orion glows with the light of newborn stars. Earth-based telescopes do not show whether the stars have planets.

After about a million years, the gale died down. Many changes lay ahead for the four inner planets. Their molten rocks would give off gases, which formed new atmospheres. In time the rock would cool and harden into crust. The same planets would be bombarded and scarred by huge rocks left over from the formation of the solar system. But a new star—the sun—with a family of new planets had come into being. And the third planet from the sun was to become our home. It was to become the remarkable planet Earth, from which we look out and set out into space.

The sun looks to us like a bright round ball. But when the glaring central disk is blacked out, as in the photograph below, the sun's atmosphere, or corona, can be seen. Its shape changes from day to day, and sometimes it swells up and shoots hot streams of matter across millions of miles.

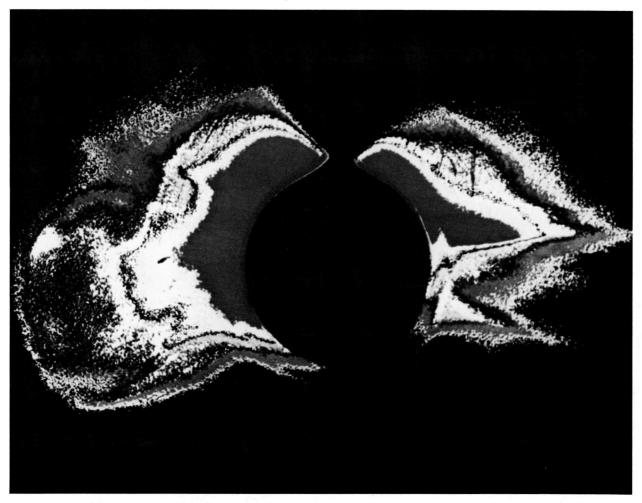

Many of the stars in this cloud in the constellation Monoceros are just beginning to shine. Careful observation of these and other very young stars shows that they produce gale winds that blow away dust and gas from their surroundings (OPPOSITE PAGE).

Because the moon takes the same amount of time to spin once that it does to orbit the earth, it always keeps the same face turned toward us. Before the space age, no one had ever seen the far side of the moon. A third of it shows (bottom, left) in this photograph taken by APOLLO 17 *astronauts.*

FIRST STOP
THE MOON

TH E moon is our closest neighbor in space. It formed about the same time as the earth and out of the same materials. Yet it is a strangely different world from ours. The chief reason is that the moon has no atmosphere. Its gravity is too weak to hold one.

The moon's sky is always black and there is no dawn or dusk, for there is no atmosphere to scatter light. As a day begins on the moon, the sun's corona appears above the horizon, followed by arching flames of gas. At last the sun's disk climbs very slowly into view. It looks colder and bluer than it does from Earth. Turn away from the sun and you will see bright stars shining in the black sky.

With no atmosphere to carry sound, the moon is completely silent. No matter what happens, there is never a sound to be heard.

If the moon ever had surface water, it has long since disappeared. Without an atmosphere, water turns to vapor and escapes into space.

Without water and an atmosphere, the moon has no weather. Clouds never fill its sky. Rain never falls. There is no such thing as wind, no such thing as air temperature.

There is only the moon's surface to warm up or cool off, and it is either extremely hot or extremely cold. The moon takes roughly 28 Earth days to spin once on its axis. So periods of daylight and darkness each last about two weeks. One side of the moon bakes in the sun's unfiltered rays for 14 days while the other lies in the cold of night. The heat is very hot and the cold is very cold because there is no atmosphere to spread heat. By day surface temperatures rise above the boiling point of water. By night they may drop 500 degrees Fahrenheit.

On the airless moon these astronaut footprints may last a million years or more. In the background is Mount Hadley, which rises some 14,700 feet above the plain.

The far side of the moon held a surprise: lack of plains. The near side is about half covered with these plains, but the far side has almost none. The largest one appears at left and is only 220 miles wide. In science the answer to one question (What does the far side of the moon look like?) often raises a new question (Why does the far side lack plains?) that takes time to answer.

The lack of atmosphere also means that there is little erosion on the moon. The moon's surface is so old that it holds clues to the early history of the solar system. But scientists could not study the clues until space-age orbiters circled and photographed the moon, landings were made, and *Apollo* astronauts brought back samples of the moon's rocks.

The story told by moon rocks is one of violent events in ancient times, but the story is not complete. One of the mysteries is where the moon came from in the first place.

Was it torn out of the young earth? Some scientists long believed it was. But then its rocks should be the same as Earth's—and they are not. They contain the same chemical elements but in different proportions.

Was the moon a small planet that the earth captured? This idea seems unlikely. To be captured, the moon would have had to pass the earth at exactly the right distance. Too far away, it would have whipped past the earth. Too near, it would have collided with the earth.

Did the moon form out of tiny rocks that were orbiting the earth? Maybe it did, but again there is a problem. Why are the moon's rocks different from the earth's?

Bagfuls of small rocks brought back by astronauts revealed much of the moon's distant past. The APOLLO 17 *astronaut standing beside this huge boulder is holding an instrument used to measure scale and color for surface photography.*

Perhaps the moon was born when a small planet-in-the-making grazed the earth and went into orbit. Material from the earth was added to its own material. At present that idea seems the most likely explanation of the moon and its rocks.

Whatever happened, the moon grew by sweeping up rocks from its orbit. As its mass increased, so did its gravity. Stronger gravity caused huge rocks to smash into the moon at high speeds. The collisions created heat. And the heat turned the outside of the moon into a deep, white-hot ocean of molten rock.

In time the collisions grew fewer. The outside layer of the moon began to cool, giving off heat into space. The lighter materials in the molten rock rose to the top and hardened. They formed a crust. From time to time, giant chunks of rock, or meteorites, crashed into the crust and made huge craters in it.

Meanwhile, the inside of the moon had been heating up. The moon's interior, like the earth's, held certain chemical elements that are radioactive. That is, they break down and give off parts of themselves as little packets of energy. The energy takes the form of heat. Radioactive heating is slow. But over millions of years the heat can grow great enough to melt rock. That was what happened inside the moon.

Lava welled up through cracks in the crust and poured out over the surface. When gigantic meteorites hit the moon, they broke through the crust and lava erupted. Lava flows formed the large black plains that are called *maria*, or seas, because early astronomers thought they were bodies of water.

This area, named the Sea of Tranquility by early astronomers, is really a vast plain made of lava and pocked with craters.

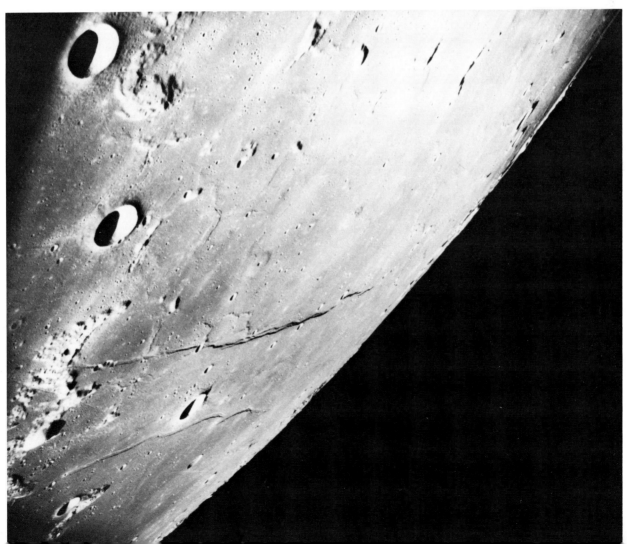

The giant crater Copernicus was formed when a huge meteorite slammed into the moon and buried itself. The impact heated rock, which flowed outward, like mud, and forced up small mountains.

After millions of years, the lava stopped flowing. The moon had given off much of its heat, and the crust had grown thick. The moon looked much as it does today. Its battered face is covered with craters, the scars of collisions, ancient and recent. It has mountains that are really the rims of craters. It has large, dark plains. A few big craters have light-colored rays pointing away from them. The rays are material that was blasted out of the craters when meteorites struck. Some of the big chunks of material made craters of their own where they fell. Probably all the big craters once had rays. But the rays of older craters have been erased by lava flows or new craters.

By studying moon rocks, scientists have been able to work out a timetable of events on the moon. All rocks contain very small amounts of radioactive elements. Because they are giving off parts of themselves, the atoms of these elements are changed. They become atoms of another element. For example, there is a variety of uranium called uranium 238. When its atoms break down, they form atoms of lead 206. Scientists know the rate at which uranium 238 breaks down: in 4.51 billion years one-half the uranium atoms will change to atoms of lead. So by measuring the number of uranium and lead atoms in a sample of rock, they can tell when the rock formed—how old it is.

In other words, radioactive elements are like clocks. As soon as molten rock hardens, its atoms are frozen in place and the clock starts to run.

The oldest rocks known come from meteorites that have struck Earth. These rocks are 4.6 billion years old, and they have not been changed by heat or erosion. So scientists feel sure that the rocks formed when the solar system did—that it is 4.6 billion years old.

The oldest moon rock that the astronauts brought back is 4.1 billion years old. It is rock that was at one time molten, and so it tells us that after the moon was born, its surface became molten. Other moon rocks show that lava stopped flowing about 3 billion years ago. Little has happened on the moon since then.

Meteorites continue to hit the moon. Some are no bigger than grains of dust and make craters, like this one, that are so tiny they can be seen only with an electron microscope. The high-speed impact of this grain of dust melted the moon rock's surface. Although the airless moon is pelted by meteorites of all sizes, the earth is not. Small bodies burn up in the atmosphere and are seen as the streaks of light called meteors.

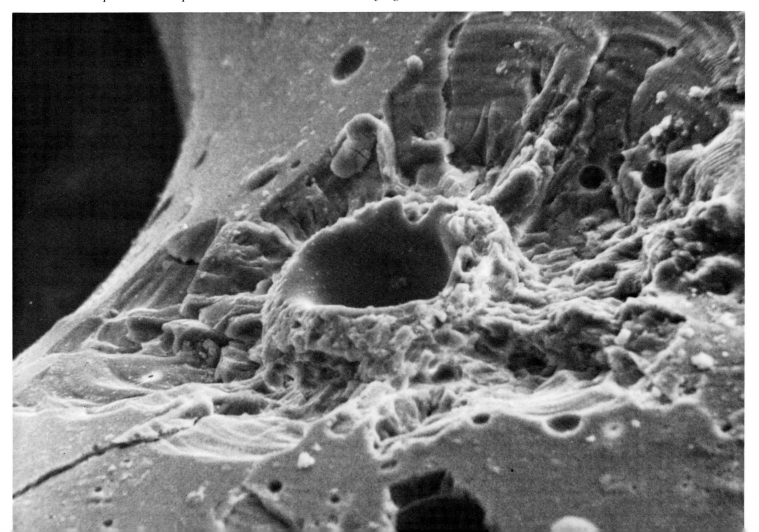

The same rocks fill in a blank page in the earth's history. The oldest known Earth rocks are 3.5 billion years old. What happened on the earth 4.1 to 3.5 billion years ago? The moon rocks tell us.

The young earth, too, was sweeping up gigantic rocks and must also have been covered by a deep sea of molten, white-hot rock. Then it slowly cooled until, after a few hundred million years, a solid crust had formed. The crust was bombarded by meteorites.

On the moon, newer craters overlap older ones and last for billions of years (OPPOSITE PAGE). *Most of Earth's ancient craters have disappeared as the surface of the earth changed. Meteor Crater in Arizona* (ABOVE) *is a recent one. It formed 15,000 to 40,000 years ago, when a chunk of iron 75 feet wide slammed into the earth and dug a crater three-quarters of a mile wide. It will probably last no more than a million years. Scientists think today's big meteorites may come from the asteroid belt.*

The young earth heated up inside. But the earth, being four times bigger than the moon, kept its internal heat—and will for millions of years. This heat is the energy that moves big plates of crust on Earth, that thrusts up mountains and makes new land. It makes Earth an active planet, the kind of planet that can support life.

The moon today appears dead. Airless, waterless, a harsh land etched in black and white, it is hostile to life. Perhaps the most beautiful sight on the moon is our blue and white planet rising in the black sky.

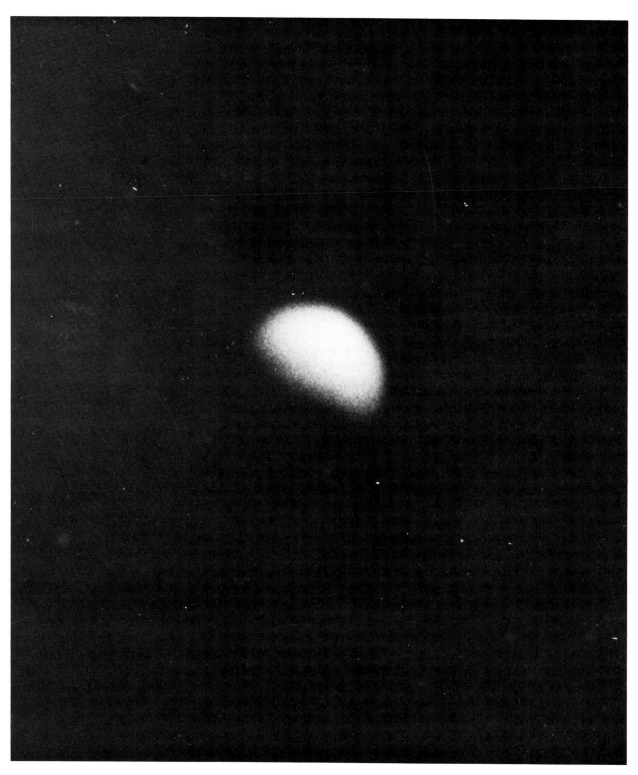

Little can be seen of Mercury through an Earth-based telescope.

MERCURY

THE FIRST CLEAR VIEW

S E E N through a telescope, Mercury looks like a badly lighted, fuzzy ball. It is a small planet, scarcely bigger than our moon, and it is also the planet closest to the sun. Its orbit lies between Earth's and the sun, and so most of the time Mercury is hidden from us by the sun's glare. It never crosses our night sky but appears briefly at certain times of the year, either just before sunrise or just after sunset. Then it is buried in the glow of dawn or twilight.

Astronomers have long known that Mercury speeds around its orbit once every 88 Earth days. By bouncing radar waves off the planet and analyzing the echoes, modern astronomers learned that Mercury spins slowly. It takes 58½ Earth days to rotate once.

But what was Mercury like? No one knew and no one could know until *Mariner 10* reached the planet in 1974. That orbiting probe gave the world its first view of the face of Mercury.

Eighteen photographs, taken at 42-second intervals, went into the making of this picture of Mercury, as MARINER 10 *approached the planet. At first glance, cratered, airless Mercury looks like the moon. The largest craters shown are about 124 miles across.*

Scientists were surprised to see that Mercury looks very much like our moon. Its face is heavily scarred with craters.

Instruments on *Mariner 10* turned up another surprise. Mercury has a weak magnetic field. Scientists had not expected to find any.

All magnetic fields are in some way caused by electric currents. (If you run a current through a wire, a magnetic field forms around it.) Earth scientists think that our planet's magnetic field comes from the molten part of its core. Earth's rapid spinning churns the molten metal and creates electric currents. The currents, in turn, create a magnetic field that spreads through the earth and into space.

Because Mercury spins slowly, scientists had thought it could not have a magnetic field. Now they wonder whether they really understand Earth's magnetic field.

A magnetic field can come only from an iron core in a planet. Scientists have calculated that Mercury's core is very big. It reaches out three-quarters of the way from the center of the planet. It is surrounded by a mantle of rock only 400 miles thick.

Discovery of the core was one of the first clues that told scientists Mercury is different from the moon, no matter what it looks like. The moon lacks both an iron core and a magnetic field. Other differences came to light as scientists studied *Mariner 10*'s photographs.

On the moon craters overlap craters. On Mercury craters are separated by smooth plains. The difference has to do with Mercury's iron core. The core gives Mercury more mass than the moon has, and so Mercury's surface gravity is stronger. Material blasted out of a crater on Mercury could not travel as far as material could on the moon. On Mercury small craters are clustered close to the main craters.

At some time a mountainous rock smashed into Mercury and broke through the crust. A sea of lava welled up. When it cooled and hardened, its waves were frozen in place.

Material blasted out of a crater on Mercury formed small craters clustered nearby. On the moon, where surface gravity is weaker, material traveled much farther.

A shallow, scalloped cliff starts near the top of the photograph and reaches hundreds of miles south.

The collision created what is called the Caloris Basin, an 860-mile-wide basin ringed by mountains.

That big collision must have shaken the whole planet. On the far side of Mercury the surface is strangely rippled with thousands of lumpy hills. Scientists think shock waves passed through the planet and came together here. The ground shook so violently that mile-high hills were pushed up in only seconds.

Mercury also has a number of shallow, scalloped cliffs, about a mile high and a few hundred miles long. No such cliffs have been seen on the moon. The cliffs are giant wrinkles in the crust. They probably formed when Mercury's iron core cooled and shrank, much as an apple's skin wrinkles when the flesh dries up.

This first glimpse leaves much still to be learned about Mercury. It seems likely, though, that little has happened on Mercury for the past 3 billion years. By then the rain of giant meteorites had ended. Lava had ceased to flow. And the atmosphere, if Mercury ever had one, had long since boiled away in the heat of a sun that looms nine times larger in Mercury's sky than in ours. Mercury had become what it is today: an airless, silent, cratered planet, baking under a huge sun in a jet black sky.

The semicircle of cratered mountains forms half the boundary of the Caloris Basin, created when a huge meteorite smashed into Mercury (OPPOSITE PAGE). The basin's name comes from the Latin word for "heat." The area is sometimes the hottest part of Mercury, with temperatures of 800 degrees.

Venus is the second planet from the sun. Its orbit is twice as big as Mercury's, and so we see it farther from the sun and more clearly. Its clouds make Venus brighter than anything in our sky except the sun and moon.

VENUS

BENEATH THE CLOUDS

F O R years Venus was believed to be the planet most like our own. It was both our next-door neighbor and an Earth-sized planet that could hold an atmosphere. The atmosphere even had clouds. The clouds reflected sunlight brilliantly and made Venus one of the brightest and loveliest objects in our sky. The same clouds hid the surface, but people guessed that it must have streams and plant life and perhaps Venusians— that it was, in fact, much like Earth, only warmer because it was closer to the sun.

Today we know that nothing could be further from the truth. Venus is indeed an Earth-sized planet with an atmosphere, but it is not Earth's "cloudy twin." Its atmosphere is carbon dioxide. The swirling upper clouds are poisonous sulfuric acid. And the rocky surface of Venus is hotter than a self-cleaning oven, which at 800 degrees turns the remains of food into fine dust. On Venus rocks glow red, like the coils on an electric range. Lightning flashes and rain falls but never reaches the surface.

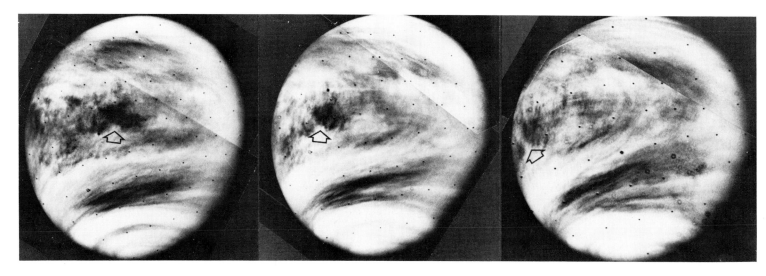

Rapid movement of Venus's clouds was recorded as MARINER 10 *flew by on its way to Mercury. Dots are not part of the atmosphere. They are engravings on the camera lens.*

This modern picture of Venus comes from modern Earth-based instruments, from flybys and orbiters, and from probes launched by the United States and the Soviet Union.

Beneath the clouds is a slowly rotating planet with an iron-nickel core and a rocky mantle and crust. Venus takes 243 Earth days to spin once on its axis, which is 17 days longer than the planet takes to orbit the sun. Stranger yet, Venus rotates backward: from east to west. On Venus the sun rises in the west and sets in the east. Although this discovery was made some 20 years ago, no one can explain it.

The layers of clouds that blanket Venus are not like Earth's white clouds of water droplets. Venus's yellowish clouds are made of droplets of sulfuric acid that is strong enough to burn human skin. At the cloud tops, some 40 miles above the surface, temperatures are chilly, a little colder than those of a home freezer. Winds of 220 miles an hour—greater than hurricane force—carry the clouds around the planet once every four Earth days.

Probes descending through the clouds meet a second layer several miles lower. Temperatures are much warmer here, and the clouds hold lots of tiny particles of some kind. No one yet knows what they are. These particles and drops of sulfuric acid rain gently down through the clouds. It is always raining sulfuric acid all over Venus, but no drop ever reaches the surface. Some 25 miles above the surface, where all the clouds end, temperatures are very high. The heat breaks up the sulfuric acid into lighter materials that are driven back up into the clouds.

Below the clouds the atmosphere is crystal clear and clean. Even so, the surface of

Venus cannot be seen from the bottom of the clouds. The air is too dense—its molecules of gas are packed together. They bounce sunlight around, so that images from the surface are lost. Trying to look through the thick air would be like looking through water.

At the surface of Venus, the atmosphere is crushing. The pressure is 90 times as great as the pressure at sea level on Earth. It is as great as the pressure 3,000 feet down in the ocean.

There is plenty of light on Venus, about as much as Earth has on an overcast day. But light rays are bent by the dense atmosphere, as they are by a prism. So the horizon rises like the rim of a bowl. The sun coming up in the west appears greatly flattened and stretched out. Nothing can be seen clearly that is more than 100 yards away.

Winds at the surface are light, perhaps two miles an hour, but powerful because the air is dense. They have the force of a current in a river.

The temperature at the surface is about 900 degrees. That is hot enough to melt tin, lead, and zinc. It is hotter than the surface temperature of sun-baked Mercury. So much heat is trapped by the atmosphere of Venus that even the nightside of the planet doesn't cool off much. It is hotter than we can imagine, with eerily glowing rocks.

Because of the acid clouds and the great heat, space probes do not survive long on Venus. But two Soviet probes lasted long enough to send back one photograph each of their landing sites. The photographs show a surface strewn with eroded rocks.

Recently we have learned much more about the surface of Venus through radar. The United States put into orbit *Pioneer Venus 1*. It carried a special kind of radar instrument that could measure land forms and make images of what it found. The result is a map covering 93 percent of Venus's surface. Venus has a mountain higher than Everest, two big plateaus—one with a giant rift valley—and shield volcanoes bigger than the chain

The first photograph of Venus's surface was taken by the Soviet probe VENERA 9. *The rocks are about 12 to 16 inches long. The horizon can be seen in the upper right.*

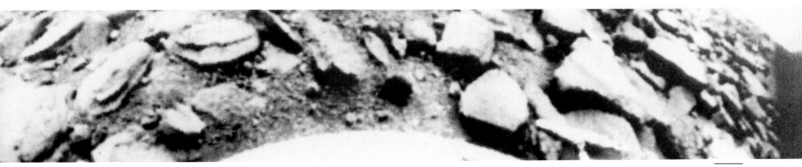

that forms the Hawaiian Islands. Two towering volcanoes seem to erupt constantly, triggering bolts of lightning in the sky. Most of Venus is made up of gently rolling uplands. It has nothing like the ocean basins that cover more than two-thirds of the earth.

So far, no one knows how the surface of Venus took shape. The map does not show signs of big plates of crust. Nor does it show craters, perhaps because they are too small for the radar mapper to find or perhaps because there are none. It will take another orbiter with an even better radar mapper to show the surface of Venus in greater detail. The detail is important. It will help us understand why Venus and Earth long ago became such different planets.

As of today, the big difference is in their atmospheres. Earth's atmosphere is nearly 80 percent nitrogen and 20 percent oxygen, with traces of water vapor, carbon dioxide,

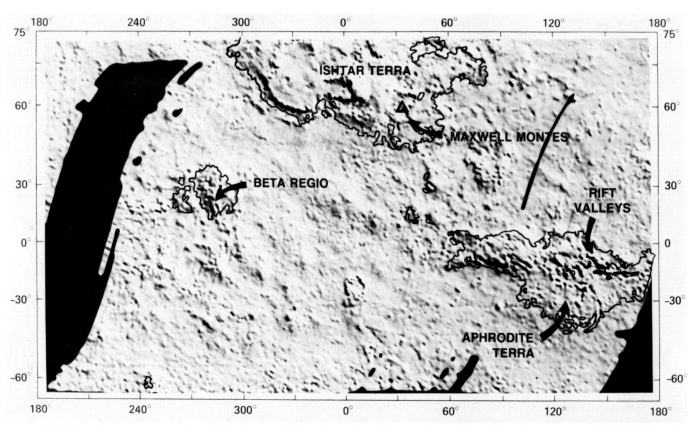

A U.S. radar mapper produced this image of Venus's surface. The northern hemisphere has a mountainous region that contains Maxwell Montes, a mountain higher than Mount Everest. It overlooks Venus's highest plateau, Ishtar Terra, which is about the size of Australia. Beta Regio is a region of shield volcanoes, perhaps the biggest in the solar system. Aphrodite Terra is another big plateau, half the size of Africa, with a rift valley 3 miles deep, 175 miles wide, and 1,400 miles long. Black areas represent gaps in the coverage. The smallest images the mapper could show were about 60 miles wide.

An artist's drawing shows the highest point yet found on Venus, Maxwell Montes. Taller than Mount Everest, Maxwell occupies the east end of Ishtar Terra.

An artist's drawing of what Aphrodite Terra and its rift valley may look like.

and other gases. The water vapor and carbon dioxide trap just enough of the sun's heat to keep the earth warm, to keep the oceans liquid, to make life possible on Earth.

Venus's atmosphere is nearly 97 percent carbon dioxide and 3 percent nitrogen, with tiny traces of water vapor, oxygen, and other gases. The carbon dioxide and water vapor trap nearly all the sun's heat on Venus.

Venus is an almost perfect greenhouse. Earth is not, which is just as well for us and other forms of life.

But why are the atmospheres different? That is the question scientists would like to answer. They think that long ago the young earth had an atmosphere that was rich in carbon dioxide. As time passed, most of the carbon dioxide was taken out of the air. Much combined with materials in the earth's crust to form rock such as limestone. Plants took carbon dioxide out of the air, used it to make food, and gave off oxygen. Sea creatures took carbon dioxide out of the oceans and used it to make their shells. The earth's atmosphere became what it is today.

Why didn't the same thing happen on Venus? Did Venus never have water, which is needed for carbon dioxide to make limestone? Or did heat make the difference? Young Venus may have been 50 degrees warmer than young Earth. A higher temperature makes it harder for rocks to take carbon dioxide out of the air. Perhaps young Venus was too hot to develop the way Earth did. When we understand Venus better, we will understand Earth better—and how to keep it the way it is.

Cloud-covered Venus holds clues to the past, present, and perhaps the future of Earth.

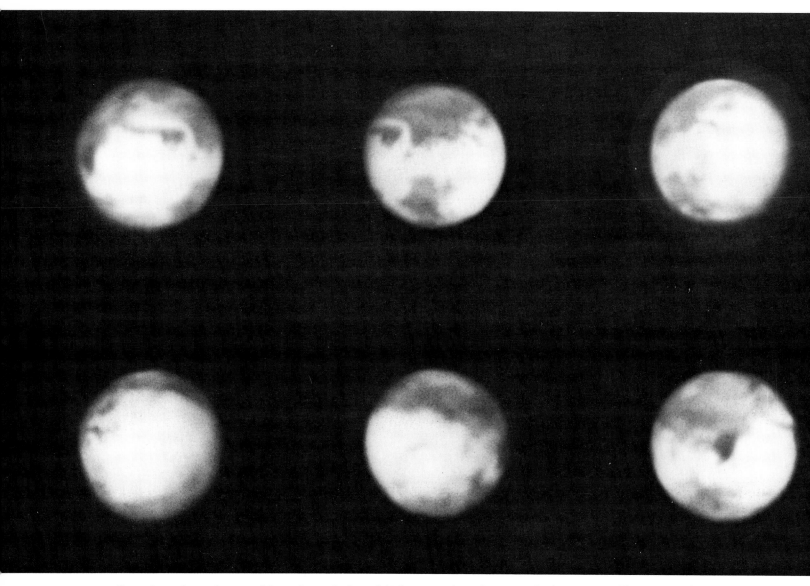

Seen through a telescope, Mars shows dark and light areas that change with the seasons. This series of pictures shows the entire surface of the planet. South is at the top because a telescope turns an image upside down.

MARS

A CLOSE-UP PICTURE

IS there life on Mars? Was there ever life on Mars? The possibility catches the imagination. In many ways Mars seems a likely place to look for life, past or present.

Fourth planet from the sun, Mars is like Earth in many ways. It is smaller than the earth and reddish, because of some kind of rusted iron in its soil. But it has an atmosphere in which white clouds appear, and it has polar ice caps. Since its axis is tilted at the same angle as Earth's, Mars has seasons in its northern and southern hemispheres. They last nearly twice as long as Earth's, because Mars is farther from the sun. It travels a bigger orbit at slower speeds, taking 687 Earth days to make one trip around the sun. Its day, however, is just a little longer than ours.

Mars, like Earth, is a planet on which changes take place with the seasons. Each ice cap grows in winter and shrinks in summer. Colors change. Seen even blurrily through a telescope, the dark markings of spring and summer turn pale as winter approaches.

Mars is like the earth in another way. Among the inner planets, only Mars and Earth have moons. Mars has two tiny, potato-shaped moons, named Phobos and Deimos.

About a hundred years ago, some astronomers began seeing straight lines on Mars.

The more they studied Mars, the more lines they saw crisscrossing the planet in a network. Since straight lines were obviously the work of intelligent beings, imaginations leaped ahead. The lines must be canals, dug to move water from melting polar ice caps to croplands near the equator. What had forced the Martians to dig these canals? There was only one answer. Mars was slowly drying up. It was a dying planet whose desperate inhabitants had tried to buy time.

Today no one knows what those earlier astronomers were seeing. Modern astronomers have never seen straight lines on Mars—but they have seen changing colors that hinted of plant life.

The first flybys put an end to hopes of finding widespread plant life on Mars. Photographs showed a cratered landscape that looked more like the moon than like Earth. But on Mars the craters were flat-bottomed and appeared to be filled with dust. Instruments reported on the carbon dioxide atmosphere. It was very thin; air pressure was less than one one-hundredth the air pressure on Earth at sea level. Because the atmosphere was thin, the carbon dioxide did not create a greenhouse effect. Temperatures on most of Mars were well below the freezing point of water. During a polar winter, temperatures fell below minus 200 degrees. At such levels, carbon dioxide freezes into ice, the kind called dry ice on Earth. A polar ice cap grew on Mars when carbon dioxide froze out of the atmosphere as dry ice. It shrank when temperatures rose, and the ice turned into gas.

Was Mars then, just like the moon, only with ice caps? The answer turned out to be no, not at all. It came from the photographs taken by *Mariner 9*, which went into orbit around Mars, and from those taken by two *Viking* orbiters and the landers that sent back the first pictures from the surface of Mars.

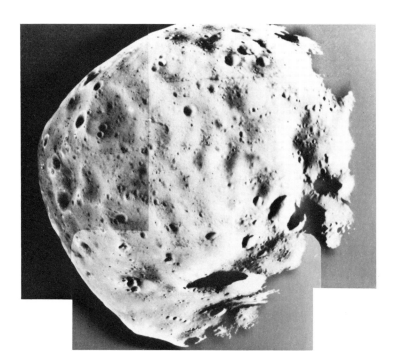

Mars has two tiny moons that orbit their planet close to its equator. The larger moon, Phobos (shown here), measures about 13 miles across and 12 miles from top to bottom. Its many craters suggest that it is very old. Scientists are not sure where the moons came from. They may have formed from collisions of tiny rocks that orbited Mars in the distant past. Or they may be asteroids that wandered too close to Mars and were captured.

Olympus Mons, the largest known volcano in the solar system, was built by countless flows of lava, as were the Hawaiian Islands. The steep cliffs at its base were probably carved by wind erosion.

Mariner 9 arrived in the middle of a planet-wide dust storm. When the dust finally settled, *Mariner 9* began sending back pictures that took scientists by complete surprise. No one had ever imagined that Mars might look as it did.

The first thing to come into sight was the top of a gigantic volcano, the biggest anyone had ever seen. Named Olympus Mons, this giant is the biggest mountain so far known in the solar system. It towers three times as high as Mount Everest. Its broad, cliff-edged base would barely fit between San Francisco and Los Angeles.

Olympus Mons is one of four huge volcanoes that rise from the Tharsis Plateau at the equator of Mars. Tharsis itself would more than cover the United States from Los Angeles to New York. It is a huge dome-shaped bulge in the crust.

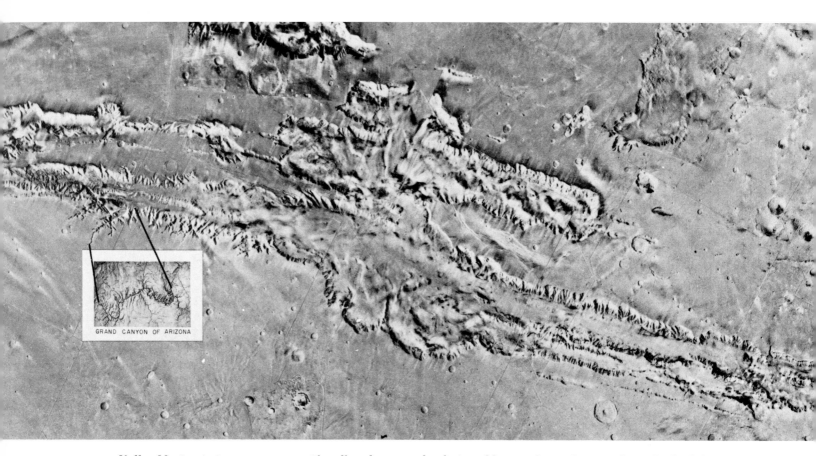

GRAND CANYON OF ARIZONA

Valles Marineris is an enormous rift valley that cuts deeply into Mars and stretches nearly a third of the way around the planet. It is more than 3,000 miles long. One of its small branch canyons is about the size of Earth's Grand Canyon. In the close-up view, the far wall of the main canyon clearly has had several landslides, perhaps triggered by marsquakes. The near side widens into branch channels. These may have formed when the ground thawed and material slid downhill. Or they may have formed when water eroded the surface.

Some 3,000 miles away is another group of big volcanoes. For unknown reasons, most of the volcanoes on Mars are in the northern hemisphere, while most of the craters are in the southern hemisphere. By chance, the flybys photographed only parts of the southern hemisphere.

To the east of Tharsis is an enormous rift valley, called Valles Marineris. It starts as jumbled land and becomes a canyon that is three times as deep as Arizona's Grand Canyon and so long that it would span the United States from coast to coast.

How did the valley form? One idea is that it marks a place where two huge plates of crust began to move apart. Since Mars is a small planet, it may have lost heat so quickly that nothing more happened. Another idea is that heat inside Mars made it expand, tearing the crust apart. Whatever happened, it is clear that Mars has been—and perhaps still is—hot inside. At times, molten rock has poured out, building giant volcanoes.

Large parts of Mars are covered with fine dust. In some places the dust forms dunes, like the sand dunes in Earth's deserts. The dust moves with the winds. It has filled in crater bottoms. It erodes and carves rock. And it accounts for the color changes seen on Mars.

Dust storms occur seasonally on Mars. When a storm ends, surface colors have changed. Light-colored dust covers areas that were dark. In other areas, winds have stripped away the dust, revealing darker material.

The winds of Mars move dust around the planet, burying some areas and exposing others. The boulder at left, nicknamed Big Joe, was once probably entirely hidden by dust and later dug out by the wind.

The first photograph ever taken on the surface of Mars shows sand or dust and rocks pitted by erosion. The large rock in the center is about four inches wide. The object in the lower right is a footpad of the VIKING 1 lander.

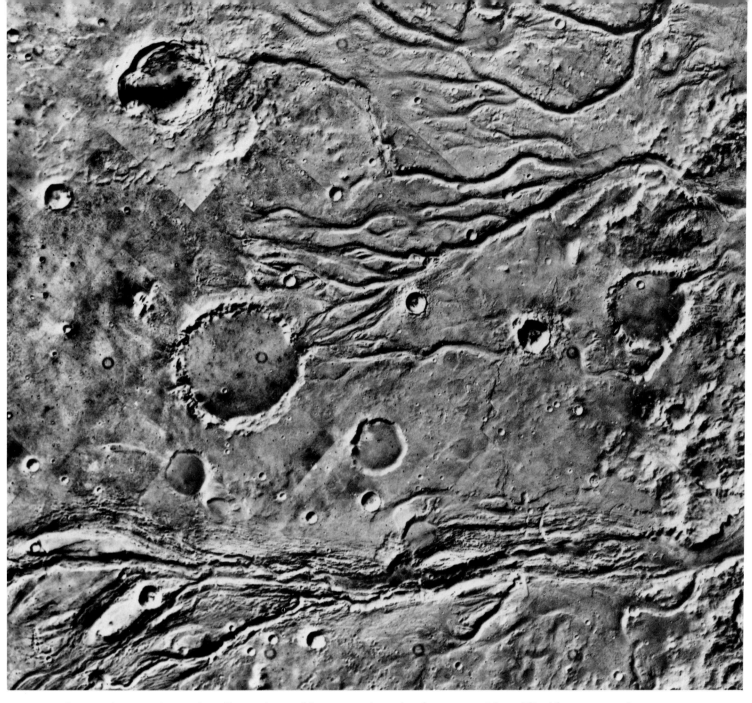

Among the most interesting discoveries on Mars were signs that large quantities of liquid water may have swept across its surface in the past. Dry channels weave down slopes and look like riverbeds. Some cut through craters, showing that the craters formed first. Others are broken by craters that formed later. The channels in this photograph flow to the right.

Because the surface of Mars is bone dry, no one expected to see signs of ancient floods. Yet parts of the surface appear to have been shaped by streams and flash floods. There are places that look as if they had once been a sea of mud. This discovery was perhaps the biggest surprise of all.

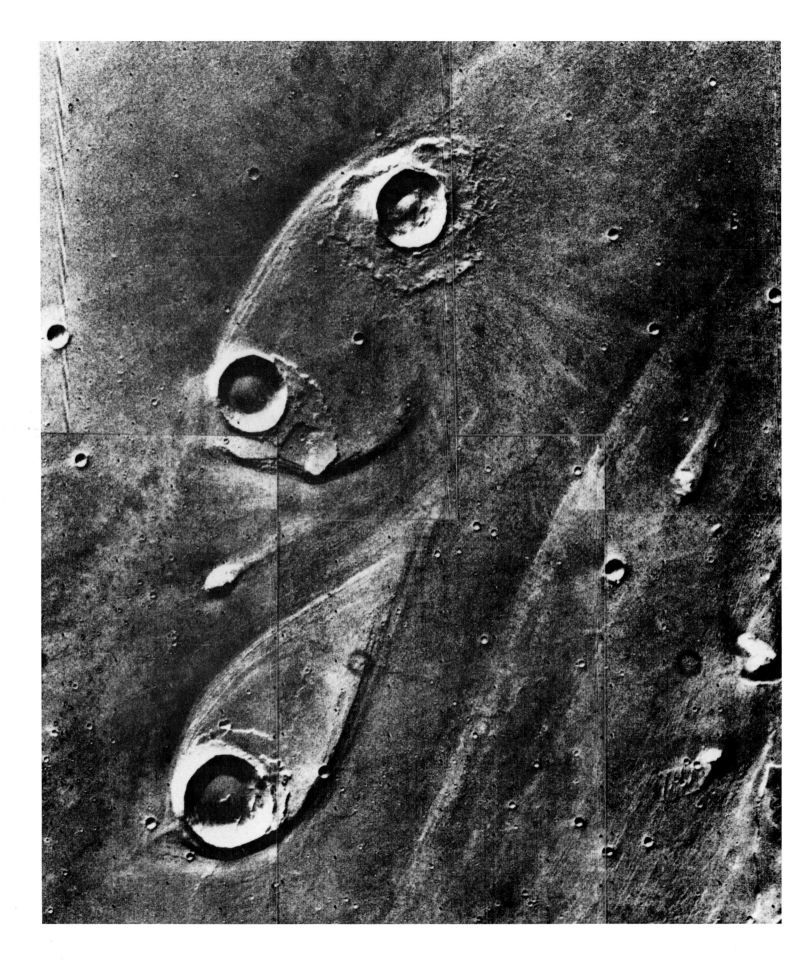

Where could water have come from? The answer has to be, from Mars itself.

There are traces of water vapor in the planet's atmosphere. But even if it could all condense and fall as rain, there's not enough to cause a flood.

A fresh young crater, lower right, about 18 miles in diameter, lies near a dry river channel that runs along a cliff.

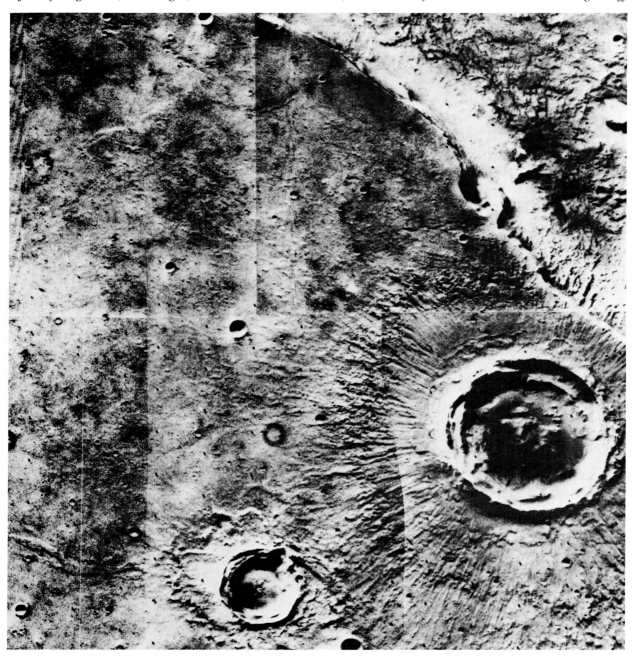

Millions of years ago a flash flood apparently swept over part of the Chryse plains (OPPOSITE PAGE), *wiping out everything except a few high-rimmed craters.*

There is water ice in the polar ice caps. Each pole has a year-round ice cap to which frozen carbon dioxide is added in winter. The north polar cap is made entirely of water ice, mixed with dust. The south polar cap seems to be made mostly of water ice and perhaps some frozen carbon dioxide.

Much more water is frozen in the ground, near the surface. It is like the permafrost of Earth's arctic regions.

And recent radar studies seem to show that a few parts of Mars have underground supplies of liquid water.

In one form or another, water does exist on Mars. But at present liquid water cannot exist on the surface. The air pressure is too low and the temperature too cold. Any liquid water would turn to vapor or to ice.

Suppose, though, there was a time when Mars was warmer. Less carbon dioxide would be locked up as ice. More would be in the atmosphere, and air pressure would increase. The carbon dioxide in the air would trap most of the sun's heat. The heat would melt water ice and permafrost. Floods of water might then occur. Water could stay liquid with warmer temperatures and greater air pressure.

Two things could make Mars warmer, some scientists suggest. One is an increase in heat from the sun itself; our star is a steady producer of light and heat, but changes do take place in its output. The other is a change in the tilt of Mars's axis; such changes do occur, caused by the pull of Jupiter and other planets. Perhaps in the past some parts of Mars received more heat than they do today. If these scientists are right, then Mars has had periods of being warmer and wetter than it now is.

If Mars has water, has it also had life? We don't know. The *Viking* landers carried out experiments to look for life in the soil. None was found. But that does not prove there has never been life on Mars. It does not prove there is no life on Mars. The landers looked for it in only two places. Besides, the experiments may have asked the wrong questions. They may have looked for the wrong kind of life.

Understanding Mars is important for us. Earth has had warm periods and cold periods. There have been times when, in the cold parts of the earth, more snow fell than the summer sun could melt. The snow packed down into ice that built up into glaciers. And the glaciers advanced over large parts of the earth. No one knows for sure why this happened. But we do know that the tilt of Earth's axis is slightly affected by Jupiter and other planets. We also know that Mars and Earth share the same sun. Our histories are twined together. Clues to our own past and future may lie in the ice caps of Mars, for thick ice holds a record of past climates.

This globe of Mars is made from more than 1,500 television pictures taken by MARINER 9. *The year-round north polar ice cap is at the top of the globe. It is made of many layers of water ice and dust, carved by the wind into steep cliffs, or terraces. The ice may hold clues to changes in Mars's climate—and also in Earth's.*

JUPITER
SOME GIANT SURPRISES

B E Y O N D Mars are the asteroids, the belt of rocks, some as big as mountains, that orbit the sun. Beyond the asteroids is Jupiter, first and biggest of the four giant outer planets. As befits a giant, exploration of Jupiter turned up some giant surprises: a ring that no one had ever even glimpsed and moons unlike any others known.

A giant among giants, Jupiter is truly enormous. Eleven Earths could be lined up along its diameter. More than a thousand Earths would fit inside it. Jupiter contains twice as much material as all the other planets together. It is so big and bright in our sky that it can easily be seen without a telescope. Through even a small telescope, it appears as big as the moon does to the unaided eye.

We see only the top of Jupiter's atmosphere. It is a churning sea of colored clouds— pink, tan, yellow, blue-green, gray. Many stretch around the planet in bands. The top of the atmosphere is also marked by plumes, streaks, spots, and patches that range in color from white to red to reddish brown.

Traveling around a nearly circular orbit, Jupiter takes almost 12 years to make one trip around the sun, but it rotates once in slightly less than 10 Earth hours. This rapid rate of spinning gives Jupiter the shape of a slightly flattened ball (OPPOSITE PAGE).

The *Pioneer* flybys found that the light-colored bands form bulges in Jupiter's atmosphere. They are places where extra-large amounts of air are piled up. The extra weight causes high pressure farther down in the atmosphere. The dark-colored bands are low-pressure regions, with less-than-average amounts of air. Just as water flows downhill, so air flows from highs to lows.

Beneath its cloud deck, Jupiter is a hot planet; it gives off twice as much heat as it receives from the sun. Scientists think the heat is left over from the time when Jupiter formed. The heat warms gases, which rise in the atmosphere. Winds, caused by the planet's rapid spin, stretch the rising gases into long bands of high pressure. But the top of the atmosphere is a chilly 200 degrees below zero. The warm gases cool and flow into the low-pressure bands. They descend through the atmosphere, are heated, and rise again.

The colors remain mysterious. No one yet knows what they are, where they come from, or why they don't all mix together. Jupiter is made mostly of hydrogen and helium, which are colorless gases, with traces of other gases that are also colorless. Some scientists think the colors must come from chemicals of some kind. Perhaps the chemicals change color when they are acted on by lightning in Jupiter's atmosphere. Perhaps they change when acted on by sunlight, somewhat in the way a person's skin tans when acted on by sunlight.

Another mystery of Jupiter's atmosphere is the Great Red Spot. It was first seen in 1655, but no one knows when it first appeared. It is a big, reddish, football-shaped, swirling mass of gas that has changed color and size as astronomers have watched it over the years. The spot varies from brick red to grayish red. Sometimes it is so big you could line up three Earths across it. At other times it shrinks by a third. The Great Red Spot revolves around Jupiter along with other cloud features, but it travels more slowly. It also spins on its own axis about once every seven Earth days. It may be some sort of storm.

Astronomers have long known that Jupiter has a magnetic field, because the planet gives off continuous radio static. There are also great bursts of radio noise, caused by lightning. The *Pioneer* flybys showed that Jupiter's magnetic field is ten times stronger than Earth's. The *Voyager* flybys showed the field's size. It is bigger than the sun itself. Vast numbers of charged particles from the sun are trapped by the field, creating a sea of deadly radiation.

Scientists feel sure that Jupiter has no solid surface beneath its clouds. It has an atmosphere that is mostly hydrogen gas. Deeper down, where the pressure of the atmosphere is very great, the molecules of gas are pushed together, or compressed. They are so compressed that they form a liquid. This layer of liquid hydrogen is 43,000 miles deep.

Beneath that layer, pressures are believed to be 3 million times the air pressure on Earth, the result of trillions and trillions of tons of matter pressing downward. Here the hydrogen may be so compressed that it acts like a liquid metal. There is a great, dark ocean of it, 29,000 miles deep. Here Jupiter's magnetic field is probably produced by electric currents.

Beneath the ocean of metallic hydrogen, there may be a solid core of rock and iron. If so, it is trapped in pressures we could not even imagine, at temperatures higher than those on the sun's surface.

Photographs from VOYAGER 2 *produced this picture of the Great Red Spot. It seems to be a huge storm system. Other storm systems take the form of long-lived white ovals, one of which can be seen just below the Great Red Spot. Still others appear as smaller red spots. Even the plumes may be like huge thunderstorms.*

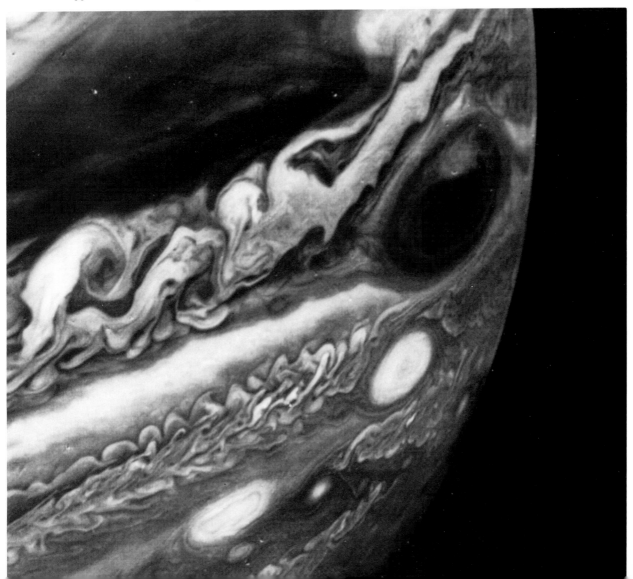

Jupiter has at least 15 moons, three of them only recently discovered. The eight small outer moons are probably asteroids that mighty Jupiter captured. Among the inner moons are four big ones: Callisto, Ganymede, Europa, and Io. Together they are called the Galilean moons, in honor of the great Italian astronomer, Galileo, who discovered them in 1610. *Voyagers 1* and *2* gave us our first good look at these moons.

CALLISTO

Callisto is the outermost of the Galilean moons, and nearly twice the size of Earth's moon. Its dark surface is ice,

Callisto is an old and battered world.

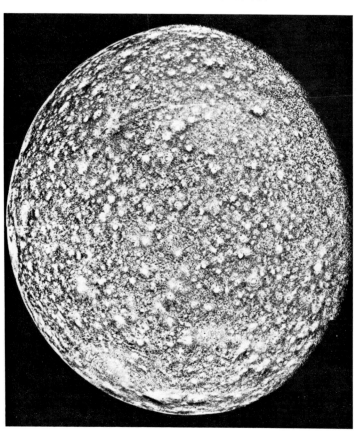

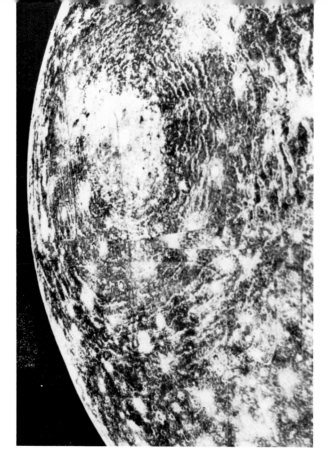

When Callisto was young, a giant meteorite crashed into it and made this 185-mile-wide basin that is surrounded by rings. The icy surface must have melted into a steamy sea that quickly refroze.

perhaps mixed with dust. Under its deep, frozen ocean is a rocky core. Callisto's battered face shows that the surface is very old. The big moon probably formed when the planets did and was bombarded by rocks and other leftover matter.

Many of the old craters have flattened out, because ice flows very slowly. There are signs of large meteorites that slammed into Callisto and briefly melted the icy crust. The dark surface suggests that dirt has been left behind as ice turned to vapor and drifted away. Recent craters are marked by bright rays, but Callisto looks much as it did 4 billion years ago.

GANYMEDE

The next moon is Ganymede, Jupiter's biggest moon. At first glance, Ganymede looks very much like our moon. It is peppered with craters and has large dark patches. But the dark areas are not plains, as they are on our moon. They are cratered crust, broken by bands of strange grooves and ridges that look as if they had been made by a giant rake. The grooves are hundreds of miles long, a few miles wide, and about a hundred yards deep. The ridges are about 3,000 feet high. Nothing like the grooves and ridges has been seen anywhere else in the solar system.

Ganymede's surface is marked by mysterious sets of grooves, with ridges thrown up beside them.

The youngest craters on Ganymede are marked by white—ice flung outward from the crater basins. Older areas are darkened by rock and dirt.

Some bands of grooves run across big craters. Some big craters lie on top of grooves. So scientists think the grooves and craters were formed in the same period of Ganymede's history. The craters must be very old, because few young craters are that big, and therefore the grooves must be very old.

What are the grooves? No one knows. Ganymede has an icy crust that may float on a layer of slush. At its center is a solid core of rock. Perhaps young Ganymede heated up inside, expanded, and tore its crust apart. Perhaps the grooves and ridges mark fractures where plates of ice moved and jostled one another. Perhaps they are signs of mountain building. For now, they remain a mystery.

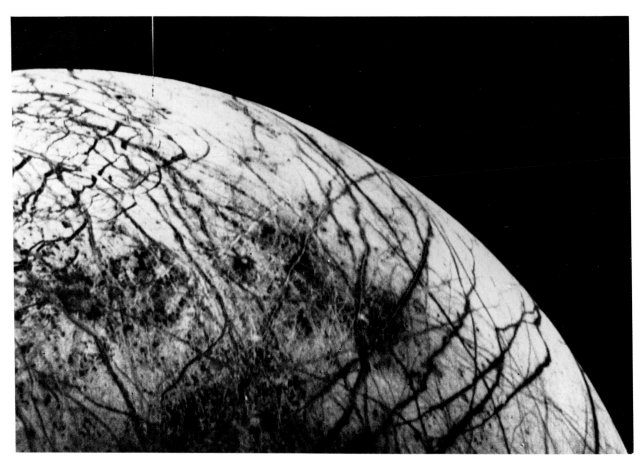

Europa's smooth ice surface lacks the giant craters seen on its outer neighbors. A few white spots on the surface may be small, recent craters. The cracks are a puzzle. They may be dark because of ground-up rock from inside the moon.

EUROPA

Europa looks like a billiard ball with cracks. Its smooth surface is ice, perhaps 60 miles thick. There are no mountains, no ancient giant craters. There are only the cracks or streaks, a dark network of lines that run on for hundreds of miles.

The smoothness suggests that the surface is young. Like its neighbors, Europa must have been bombarded by huge chunks of rock long ago. But the scars do not show. Somehow the surface has been renewed. How this happened is not understood, but one idea is that Europa was heated inside. It expanded and cracked its crust of ice. Hot springs of water erupted onto the surface and froze. Over millions or billions of years, a thick surface of ice built up, and the craters disappeared under it. If this idea is right, Europa may still be heated inside. Perhaps it has geysers that we have not seen.

Europa might be heated by radioactivity

in its rocky core. Or it might be heated by friction. Scientists think that Jupiter's strong gravity raises land tides in Europa, just as our moon raises tides in our oceans. Europa's surface heaves up and down. The pumping action stretches and compresses the inside of the moon and heats up the inner materials. That, scientists are sure, is what happens on Europa's neighbor Io, the innermost of the big moons.

I O

When the first pictures of Io were received, watching scientists were as-

Io, the innermost of Jupiter's four big moons, is dwarfed by its giant planet, even though it is as big as our moon.

Io is about the size of our moon, but that's as far as the likeness goes. Io is hot inside, an active moon where sulfur erupts out of volcanoes.

tounded. "It looks like a pizza!" one of them said. Io was mostly orange-red with large white patches and small dark spots.

Before the arrival of *Voyager 1*, scientists had known that Io was red, redder even than Mars. They did not expect it to be red, orange, yellow, white, and black. They were also surprised not to see any craters. What could be erasing them? It couldn't be the atmosphere, because Io's escaped into space long ago. It couldn't be running water, because Io's surface temperature is too cold. The answer turned out to be the biggest surprise of all: volcanoes. In the whole solar system, no other moon is known to have active volcanoes.

65

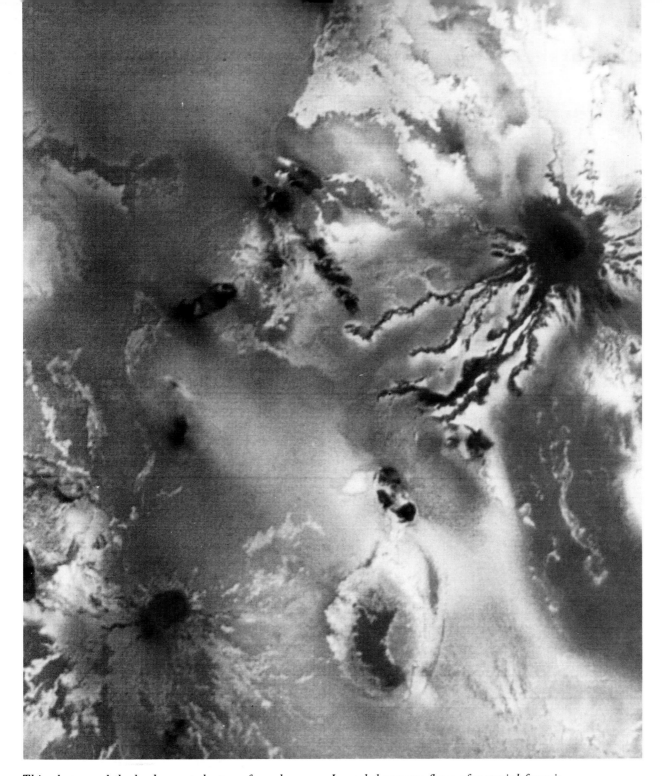

This photograph looks down at the top of a volcano on Io and the recent flows of material from it.

There are at least nine active volcanoes on Io—and hundreds of extinct ones. Their outpourings are more than enough to have buried Io's craters. Io is a moon on which the landscape is always being renewed.

VOYAGER 1 *discovered volcanoes erupting on Io. Some erupt in flows. Others, like this one, shoot out huge umbrella-shaped plumes that rise 160 miles above the surface* (OPPOSITE PAGE).

The colors of Io show that sulfur is erupting out of the volcanoes. Once molten, sulfur changes its color at different temperatures. At low temperatures it is yellowish-white. As temperatures rise, it changes from white to yellow to orange to red to black. If molten sulfur is cooled quickly, it keeps its color. On Io, plumes of molten sulfur erupt 60 or 70 miles into space, where they cool. The particles of cool sulfur fall like snow onto Io's surface.

When the volcanoes erupt, most of the material colors Io and lays down a new surface. Some of it does other things. For example, Jupiter has a tiny inner moon named Amalthea. Amalthea is potato-shaped and deep red. The color probably comes from sulfur that erupted out of Io's volcanoes, cooled, and snowed onto Amalthea.

THE RING

Another big surprise from *Voyager 1* was the discovery that Jupiter has a ring. Earth-based astronomers had never seen it. It did not appear in the photographs from the *Pioneer* flybys. But both *Voyager 1* and *Voyager 2* photographed it.

The ring is faint. The outer edge is some 34,000 miles out from the cloud tops of Jupiter. The inner edge seems to reach all the way down to the clouds. About 18 miles thick, the ring is made of fine particles that glimmer like dust specks in a beam of light. You could say that the particles are millions of tiny moons that orbit Jupiter.

The ring was not only a surprise but also a mystery that raised many questions. Where do the particles come from? Why don't they fall into Jupiter? Or, if they do fall into Jupiter, what is the source of new particles that replace old ones? The best guess is that the particles come from material thrown out by Io's volcanoes.

VOYAGER 2 *took these pictures of Jupiter's ring, looking back toward the planet.*

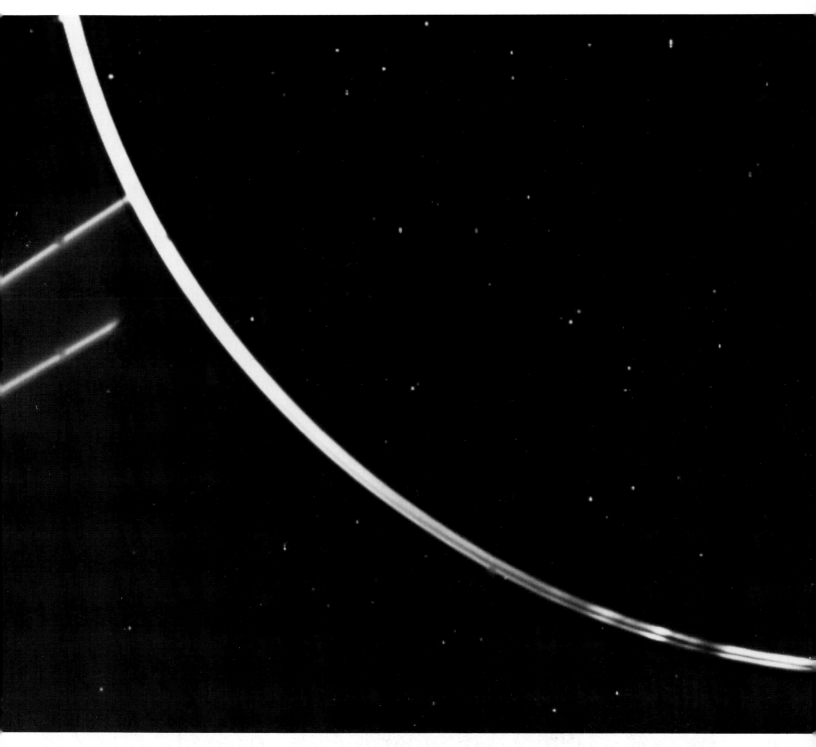

The bright rim of Jupiter is the big curve in this photograph. Two small pieces of the ring appear at left.

Saturn's rings make it the most spectacular planet in the solar system. The rings are casting their shadow on Saturn's bands of pale clouds. Part of the rings has been blacked out by Saturn's shadow.

SATURN
PUZZLE UPON PUZZLE

S A T U R N has always been a planet of puzzles. When Galileo turned his newly invented telescope toward Saturn, he was astonished to see what looked like ears on the planet—two blobs of light, one on each side of Saturn. He decided they were moons that did not move. Sometime later the "moons" mysteriously disappeared. It was a puzzle that he never solved. Later astronomers with stronger telescopes saw that the blobs of light were really rings, which disappeared when seen edge-on. There seemed to be three rings, separated by gaps. The solution to one puzzle raised a new one: Why was Saturn the only planet with rings? Today we know that it isn't. Jupiter and Uranus also have rings, and it may be that all the giant planets have rings; astronomers would not be surprised if Neptune turned out to have rings too.

But the rings are still puzzling. For one thing, scientists are not sure where Saturn's huge rings came from. Perhaps the rings are the remains of a moon that was torn apart by Saturn's gravity. Perhaps they are material of a moon that never formed, because of Saturn's gravity. Or perhaps they are something else.

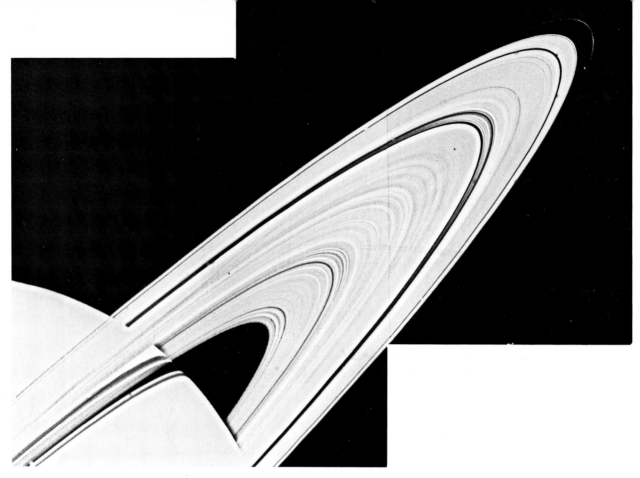

Rings within rings: Hundreds or thousands of tiny ringlets are grouped into the broader bands that make up the rings of Saturn. The faint white mark (top, right) is a newly discovered small moon that orbits outside the F ring. The black dots in this and other pictures are not part of Saturn—they come from the camera lens.

Whatever they are, the rings make Saturn the most eye-catching planet in the solar system. Yet they, like Saturn itself, are hard to study from Earth. Saturn is a giant planet, second only to Jupiter, but it is twice as far from the sun as Jupiter, and so it shines with a dimmer light.

The *Pioneer* and *Voyager* flybys gave scientists their first really good look at Saturn, its rings, and its moons. The *Pioneer*s blazed the way, discovering more rings and sending back light readings used in setting the *Voyager* cameras. From the *Voyager*s came detailed photographs that piled puzzle upon puzzle.

It turned out that the big rings are made up of little rings. Hundreds, perhaps thousands, of ringlets are orbiting Saturn. Seen close up, even the "gaps" proved to be full of ringlets. No one had expected to find rings within rings, like grooves in a phonograph record.

The rings start near Saturn's cloud tops and reach out almost 200,000 miles into space. They are thin, no more than half a mile thick. And they are made of icy objects ranging in size from a fraction of an inch to chunks the size of houses.

The brightest of the big rings, the so-called B ring, has markings that look like spokes. These dark areas appear and disappear as they revolve around Saturn in the ring. The same ring gives off crackling, lightning-like discharges of electricity that are at least 10,000 times more powerful than lightning on Earth.

Two newly discovered rings look as if they were braided. In each the ringlets appear twisted together, although each has its own orbit.

How can the ringlets be twisted? What are the "spokes" and why do they appear and disappear? What keeps them from breaking up? Could they somehow be caused by the lightning? Why does the lightning occur? Just what are the rings? How did they form?

The "spokes" in Saturn's B ring can be seen revolving around the planet in this series of pictures taken about 15 minutes apart.

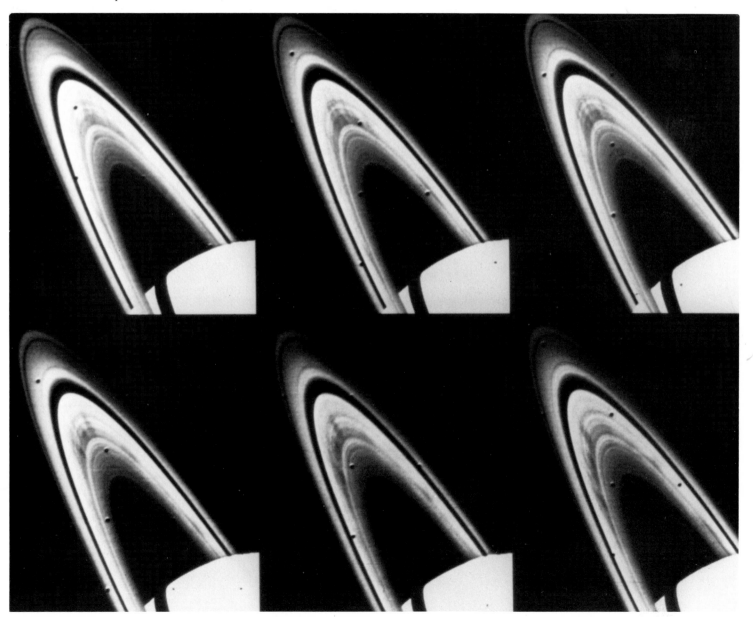

Why aren't they drawn by gravity into their planet? Why are the rings flat? Why are the ringlets grouped in big rings? Those are a few of the puzzles that will keep scientists busy for years.

For a time it seemed that *Voyager 1* might have found the answer to the last question. Among the rings, *Voyager* discovered three small moons. One orbits outside the braided F ring, and a second orbits inside that ring. Scientists think that just as sheepdogs keep a flock together these two small moons may keep material within the F ring. The third small moon seems to sheepdog the outside of the A ring. Perhaps, scientists thought, there were still more small moons that kept other ringlets grouped in big rings. *Voyager 2* looked for such moons when it flew by Saturn, but it did not find any. Perhaps there were none to be found, or perhaps the moons were too small for *Voyager*'s camera to pick up. At present the grouping of the ringlets remains a scientific puzzle.

The discovery of three new moons means that Saturn has at least 17 moons. They range in size from giant Titan, which is bigger than Mercury, to tiny moons only 50 to 60 miles in diameter.

Of them all, Titan was the most interesting to scientists. It is a planet-sized moon and the only moon known to have an atmosphere. It seemed a likely place to look for some kind of life. Scientists also hoped that *Voyager 1* would be able to see through Titan's atmosphere and return pictures of its surface. They were disappointed. Titan remained a fuzzy ball to the camera's eye.

Other instruments showed Titan to be a cold, icy body with an atmosphere of nitrogen. The clouds that hide its surface

The F ring shows narrow bright ringlets that look as if they were braided together. The "knots" that can be seen are probably clumps of ring material, but may be very small moons.

are made chiefly of poisonous methane. (Natural gas on Earth is mostly methane.) The surface temperature on Titan is nearly 300 degrees below zero. One scientist has suggested that a visitor on Titan would see little, not even rocks and craters. Everything would be buried under layers of methane ice and snow.

Saturn has several medium-sized moons with rocky cores and thick, cratered crusts of ice. They probably have not changed much since the solar system was young. For whatever reason, a moon

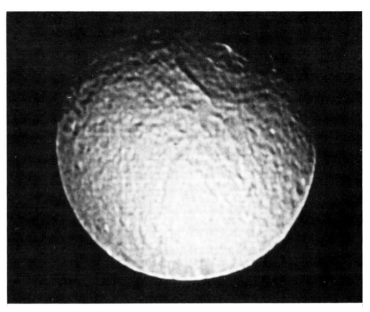

Tethys has a giant crater ringed by ice mountains. When the crater was gouged out, shock waves may have split open the far side of the moon, forming a trench 500 miles long and 40 miles wide. The crater has been flattened by the flow of ice.

named Rhea has more craters than any other moon of Saturn. Its craters stand shoulder to shoulder. Any new bombardment would destroy as many craters as it created. Tethys also has many craters. Among them is the largest, deepest crater so far seen on any of Saturn's moons. It is 250 miles wide and 10 miles deep. At its center is a tall peak, the remains of a material gouged out during the collision. Rimming the crater is a range of ice mountains that buckled out of the crust when the crater formed. Scientists think shock waves from the collision shot through Tethys and split open the far side of the moon. That side has a deep fracture that looks like a trench.

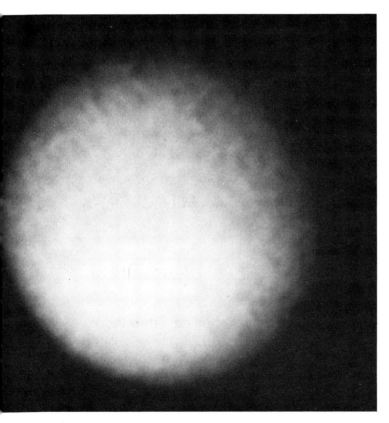

Titan seen from 7½ million miles away, remains a tantalizing ball of fuzz. The largest of Saturn's moons, it is the only moon in the solar system known to have an atmosphere.

Dione shares its orbit with a second moon. The VOYAGERS *picked up strange pinging radio noises near Saturn, of a kind not heard near any other planet. The noises are particularly clear near Dione and Tethys, both of which are inner moons.*

Mimas also bears the scar of a gigantic collision. Mimas is a small moon, only 240 miles in diameter, and the crater is 80 miles wide. No other moon has a crater that is as big in relation to its own size. Scientists are surprised that the collision didn't smash Mimas to pieces.

Saturn also has pairs of moons that share the same orbits. One pair includes Dione, which looks something like Earth's moon but is a much smaller, icy body. Dione's companion moon is called Dione B. Scientists do not know of any other

moons in the solar system that share orbits—or why Saturn's should.

It is possible that Dione raises land tides in another moon, Enceladus. Of all Saturn's medium-sized moons, only Enceladus has a surface with smooth, uncratered areas. Scientists suspect that land tides heat the moon inside and its icy craters simply melt away.

Iapetus, a large outer moon, is another puzzle. One side is icy and ten times as bright as the other side, which seems to

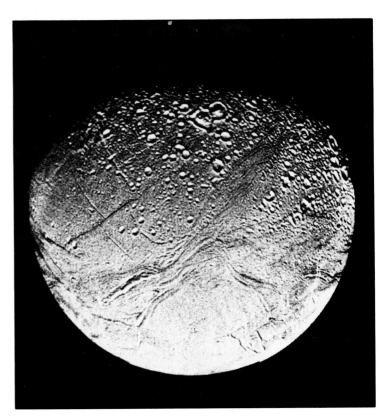

Enceladus is the smoothest of Saturn's moons. It has large areas without craters. Scientists think that internal heating melted the moon's icy crust and erased many of its craters.

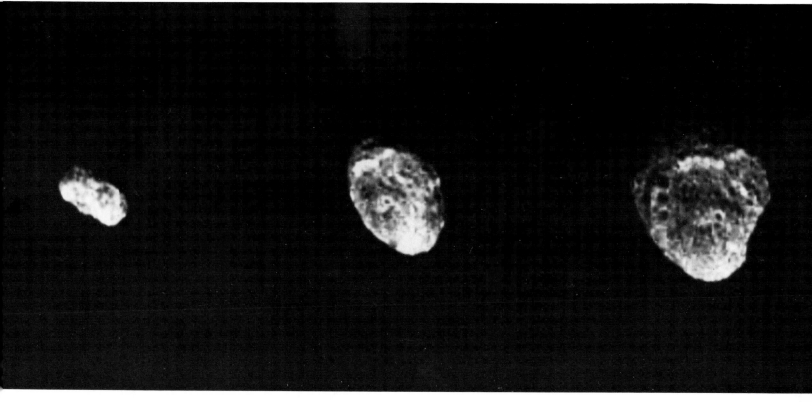

Hyperion is a small, outer moon with a big crater and a strange irregular shape. Depending on the angle from which it is viewed, it looks like a hamburger or a baking potato. Scientists think the collision that formed the big crater may have broken off parts of the moon, accounting for its strange shape.

be covered with dark material. So far scientists do not know whether the dark material comes from Iapetus or whether the moon is sweeping up dust from its orbit.

Saturn itself remains a little-known planet that is both like and unlike Jupiter. The sixth planet from the sun, it takes 29½ Earth years to complete one orbit. Like Jupiter, it spins rapidly. A day on Saturn lasts 10 hours and 40 minutes.

Iapetus has a dark hemisphere and one that is snowy bright.

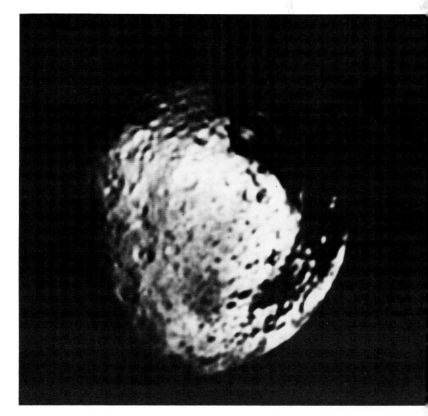

A haze of some kind partly hides the clouds of Saturn's upper atmosphere. Beneath the haze the atmosphere is somewhat quieter than Jupiter's and the clouds are paler—cream, beige, butterscotch. There are jet streams, with winds flowing at 1,000 to 1,100 miles an hour. There are storm systems that appear as blue spots and red spots. A large brown spot may be an opening in Saturn's upper cloud deck through which dark, underlying clouds can be seen. A strange feature photographed by *Voyager 2* is a big white cloud curled into the shape of a numeral 6. Placed on Earth, the 6 would reach halfway from New York to Los Angeles.

A cloud system that curls in the shape of a 6 had never been seen before VOYAGER 2 *photographed it.*

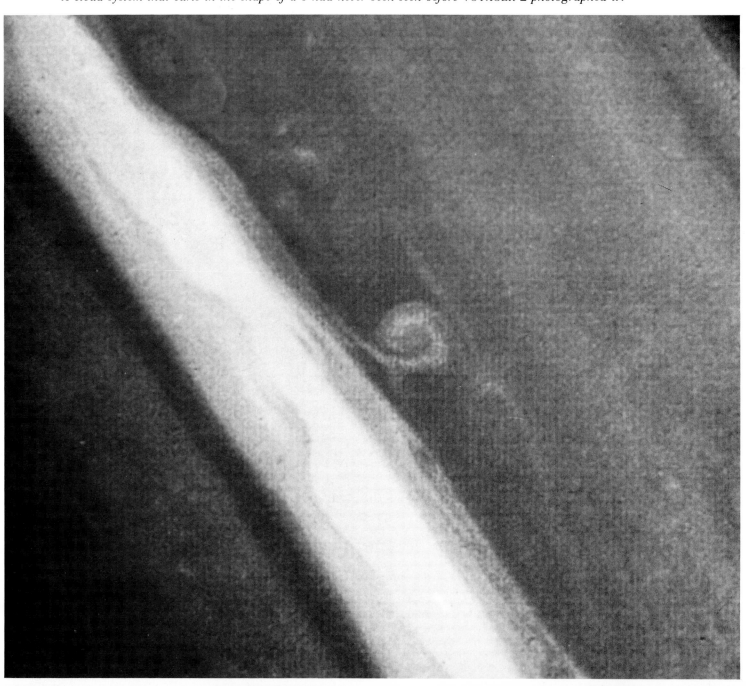

Saturn and two of its moons, Tethys (above) and Dione, were photographed from 8 million miles away. Shadows of Tethys (black dot above ring) and of the rings are cast onto Saturn's cloud tops.

What lies beneath the clouds? No one knows yet, although it seems unlikely that Saturn has a solid surface. Like Jupiter, the planet is made mostly of hydrogen and helium, but it is less dense.

Something inside Saturn produces a magnetic field. It is much weaker than Jupiter's and not even as strong as Earth's, but it is very big. Why it should be weak is still another puzzle among the many, many puzzles of Saturn.

URANUS NEPTUNE PLUTO

DARK WORLDS

IT takes very sharp eyes to see the dim gleam of Uranus in our night sky. The planet is one of the giants, but it is so far from the sun—1¾ billion miles—that it reflects little light. Even a telescope shows only a ghostly green globe.

There are times, though, when a distant planet is easier to study. These are the times when the planet, as seen from Earth, passes in front of a star and briefly cuts off the starlight. By catching the planet in action, astronomers can learn things about it.

Does the planet have an atmosphere? If it doesn't, the star will blink off instantly as the planet passes in front of it. If it does have one, the starlight will dim, little by little, disappear behind the planet, and then reappear, brightening little by little.

What is the atmosphere like? Astronomers study how the starlight behaves as it passes through the planet's atmosphere. In this way they learn about the temperature of the atmosphere, the gases in it, and its pressure.

An artist's drawing shows how Uranus looks with one pole pointed toward the sun and the other in total darkness. The rings circle its equator, as do the moons. Astronomers think that Uranus spins once on its axis every 16 or 24 hours (OPPOSITE PAGE).

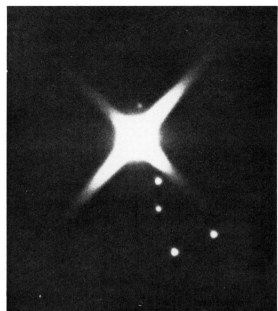

These photographs, taken over a period of time, show Uranus and its five known moons. The planet is overexposed in order to show the moons.

How big is the planet? Astronomers know the speed at which the planet is traveling. They measure the time the starlight is completely blocked. Using these two figures, they can work out the size of the planet.

In 1977 Uranus was due to pass in front of a faint star. A team of astronomers was ready to study it from an airborne observatory, a NASA airplane. In the plane they would be above 75 percent of Earth's atmosphere and its blurring effect.

As Uranus neared the star, something totally unexpected happened. The star blinked out five times. The astronomers wondered if they had discovered some unknown moons in orbit around Uranus. The planet passed in front of the star. As it moved away, the star again blinked five times. There could be only one explanation: Uranus had rings.

Nine rings are now known. They are much narrower than Saturn's and very thin. They are also dark, and that is puzzling. What are the rings made of? Why do they lack the glittering ice of Saturn's rings? Some scientists think that small sheepdog moons orbit with the rings, as they do in two of Saturn's rings. If they do, then Uranus has more moons than the five now known.

Another odd thing about Uranus is the tilt of its axis. In effect, Uranus lies on its side. For part of its year, the north pole faces the sun, then the equator does, then the south pole, and finally the equator again. Days and nights and seasons must be strange on Uranus as the planet revolves around the sun, taking 84 years to complete an orbit. At the poles, day and night each last 42 Earth years.

Beyond Uranus is Neptune, last of the giant planets. Very little is known about it. Neptune takes 165 Earth years to travel once around its big orbit, which is 30 times Earth's distance from the sun. Neptune is so dim and distant that it cannot be seen without a telescope, and a telescope shows only a faint, greenish planet with some markings in its atmosphere. Astronomers have said that trying to study Neptune from Earth is like trying to study a dime that is a mile away.

At the present time, Neptune and Uranus are thought to be near-twins. They are almost the same size: Uranus is slightly bigger but Neptune has greater mass. Both are thought to have deep atmospheres of hydrogen and helium. Methane clouds give them their greenish color. One odd difference between them is that Neptune gives off more heat than it receives from the sun, but Uranus does not. If *Voyager 2* lasts that long, it will send back the first close-up views of Uranus in 1986 and of Neptune in 1989, and knowledge of these planets will take a great leap forward.

Neptune has two known moons and a possible third. One of them, Triton, is very big. Along with Jupiter's Ganymede and Saturn's Titan, it is one of the three giant moons of the solar system. Triton has a rocky surface and a trace of methane atmosphere. The strange thing about the moon is that it orbits Neptune backward. Some small moons, probably captured asteroids, orbit their planets backward, but no other big moon does. Except for Triton, big moons move in the same direction as their planets spin. Neptune's small moon, called Nereid, is also unusual. It has a very large, oval orbit. Other moons have much more circular orbits.

The atmosphere of Neptune shows bright and dark markings. The bright regions are probably high clouds of ice crystals. The dark markings are methane clouds, which account for the planet's greenish color. Neptune takes about 18 hours to spin once on its axis.

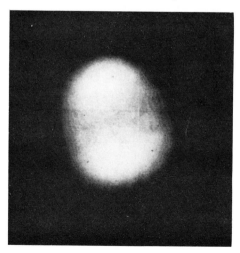 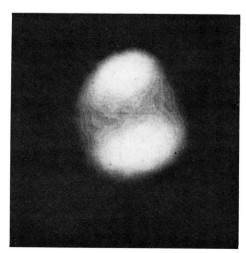 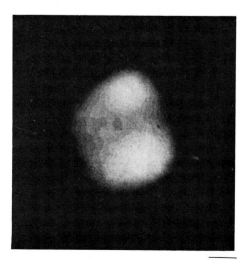

Some scientists wonder whether a great catastrophe happened in Neptune's past. Perhaps some extraordinary event accounts for these two orbits and also for Pluto.

Neptune and Pluto were discovered for the same reason. Astronomers were trying to find out why Uranus sometimes speeded up and sometimes slowed down. They thought there had to be another giant planet beyond Uranus. Its gravity must be pulling Uranus ahead faster than expected and later holding Uranus back. They worked out where the invisible planet should be, looked, and found Neptune. But even Neptune did not seem wholly to account for the movement of Uranus. Much later another search began, and Pluto was found, so far out that it takes 248 Earth years to orbit the sun.

Pluto is peculiar. Its orbit is more oval-shaped than that of any other planet. And its orbit crosses Neptune's. There are times when Pluto is closer to the sun than Neptune is.

Unlike its neighbors, Pluto is not a giant planet with a thick atmosphere. It is the smallest planet in the solar system and icy. Pluto most resembles some of the moons of its big neighbors.

Pluto itself has a recently discovered moon, named Charon. The moon is big for such a small planet, with a diameter that is nearly a third of Pluto's. Its orbit lies close to Pluto, and each always keeps the same face toward the other. They are more like a double planet than a planet and a moon.

Many astronomers think that Pluto is not a true planet, that it was not born a planet. Some suggest that it was once a moon of Neptune's, along with Triton and Nereid. All circled Neptune in normal orbits. Then some very large object passed close to Neptune. Its gravitation tore the moons out of their orbits and hurled them into new ones. Pluto was not only yanked out of its old orbit but also torn in two—it became a planet with a large moon.

Did these events ever occur? Are there clues to what happened? Might a space probe find them? We can only wait and see what new research will uncover.

Pluto's tiny size and great distance make it look like a faint star, even when photographed through a telescope. But Pluto is orbiting the sun and moving against the fixed stars. It can be identified in photographs taken only 24 hours apart, as these were. Pluto was discovered in 1930 by comparing such photographs.

OUR BLUE PLANET

O N C E small ships sailed the seas on great voyages of discovery. Today other small ships sail the sea of space, exploring the planets and their moons. Pinpoints of light in the night sky have become real places, where volcanoes erupt sulfur, where storms last hundreds or thousands of years, where the surface heat would melt tin and lead, where the sun appears as a flattened band.

These are strange worlds that fascinate everyone who sees them. Yet to the astronauts who have gone into space, the most wondrous sight of all is our own small, blue and white, ever-changing planet—a glistening outpost of life in the black of space. It is a planet to be treasured. And it is the best reason of all for exploring other planets, because the better we understand them, the better we will understand and cherish our own.

INDEX

(with pronunciation key for less familiar names)